Presented to:

_____

From:

_____

_____

Date:

_____

Christmas Remembered

Sentimental REFLECTIONS

*"Let the little children come to me, and do not hinder them,
for the kingdom of God belongs to such as these."*

—Mark 10:14

Christmas Remembered
Featuring images by Sentimental Productions.

Artwork is reproduced under license from Sentimental Productions and may not be reproduced without permission.
For information on other products featuring these charming photographs, contact:

Sentimental Productions
www.sentimentalproductions.com

For licensing information, contact
Evergreen Ideas, Inc.
(615) 826-6775

Art ©2001 by Brad Lind
Text ©2001 by Alan Cox
Production by Leisha Lindstrom

Unless otherwise indicated, all Scripture quotations are taken from the *Holy Bible, New International Version*®. NIV®.
Copyright © 1973, 1978, 1984 by International Bible Society. Used by permission of Zondervan Publishing House.
All rights reserved.

Scripture quotations marked THE MESSAGE are taken from *The Message,* copyright © by Eugene H. Peterson, 1993, 1994,
1995, 1996. Used by permission of NavPress Publishing Group.

This book was produced by Sentimental Productions. Special thanks to Melissa Cox (for lovingly enduring the long road to
reality for this project), Lynn Lind (for letting us invade your tidy home with tons of messy children), Greg Lindstrom (for
being a true friend and soul-mate under fire), and Tim O'Hare (for pouring your time and talent into this project).

This edition published by Honor Books, P.O. Box 55388, Tulsa, Oklahoma 74155.

Printed and bound in China.

ISBN 1-56292-986-0

01 02 03 04 05 06 07 08 09 10/TK/10 9 8 7 6 5 4 3 2 1

Dedicated to our children,
in whom we see
God's goodness
reflected every day.

Table of Contents

Christmas Reflections

Introduction

Mary treasured up all these things and pondered them in her heart.—Luke 2:19

What first comes to mind when you think about Christmas? Is it "the most wonderful time of year" or "the most wearisome time of the year"? For too many of us, this holiday has become far more of a headache than highlight. We get so caught up in the clamor of consumerism and the exasperation of expectations that we fail to set aside adequate time for pondering.

So take a moment now...

Remember the excitement you felt when you were a child? How eagerly you waited for the day to come? How hard it was to sleep the night before? In the wonder of their innocence, children remind us how we used to feel. Our own childhood memories are a precious treasure worth preserving.

The journaling sections in each chapter of this book invite you to reflect and record your memories of Christmas as both a child and adult. Take the time to complete these sections and share them with your kids. It will help you see Christmas again through the eyes of a child, and in so doing, reintroduce you to the wonder of Christmas. Use this book annually for recording new memories of Christmas throughout the years. You'll be creating a valuable record of your family's best Christmas traditions, experiences, and sentiments—a legacy worth passing down to your children as they begin families of their own.

In prompting you to remember your celebrations of Christmas, this book is designed to help you remember the Christ in Christmas. Each section begins by focusing on a specific part of Christmas and how it relates back to the birth or life of Jesus. Draw nearer to the meager manger, reflect on the Lord's unusual arrival, and let the wonder of it all weave its way into your thoughts just like Mary did. In doing so, you, too, will be touched by the true wonder of Christmas, and you will experience the joy of having the faith of a child.

May the God of hope fill you with all joy and peace as you trust in him.

—Romans 15:13

Once upon a time

Christmas

There once was a man

Stories

And so it came to pass

The angel said to her, "Do not be afraid, Mary, you have found favor with God. You will be with child and give birth to a son, and you are to give him the name Jesus. He will be great and will be called the Son of the Most High.

—Luke 1:30-32

Tell Me a Story...

Everybody loves a great story—especially around Christmas time. Regardless of whether it's in the form of a book, movie, or TV program, stories can warm our hearts and fire up our imaginations. And they can help us keep a healthy perspective on Christmas when the chaos of all the presents, parties, and post office lines leave us too exhausted to be of good cheer.

Perhaps you're already wondering if the spirit of the season got lost on its way to your home. Bah. Humbug. You're just a classic tale away from a new perspective. Can you honestly resist cracking a smile at the thought of Ebeneezer Scrooge and his haunting Christmas Eve visitors, Charlie Brown and his drooping tree, or George Bailey and his wonderful life? The heart-rendering stories of Christmas are special because they encourage us to change our perspective and focus on what's really important.

That was certainly the impact the Christmas Story, the story of Jesus Christ's birth, had on a young woman named Mary the first time she heard it. It was told to her by a most unusual storyteller—an angel named Gabriel. Mary was told a historical tale that was yet to take place. In this story, the Holy Spirit would come upon a virgin, and the power of the Most High would, overshadow her. Then she would give birth to the holy One, who would be called Son of God. The story itself was incredible. The fact that it was about to happen to her was unbelievable. And yet, she believed.

This would be the story of her life. Mary could have protested, dreading the probable humiliation of her unmarried pregnancy. She could have pleaded that this burden be placed upon another woman's life. She could have professed to be incapable of completing the preposterous plan. But she didn't. "I am the Lord's servant," Mary answered. "May it be to me as you have said." What a response! She understood that God was at work, and she willingly joined in the labor. Mary humbly embraced her part in this unfolding and amazing story authored by God. We each share that same opportunity for a faithful response when we hear the Christmas Story told.

Touched by a Tale or Two

If reading the accounts in Matthew 1:18-2:12 and Luke 1:5-2:40 is not already a family Yuletide tradition, make it one from this year out. Elect a family member to read the Christmas Story aloud to the rest of the family, and when the reading is finished, pause to put yourself in the place of Mary for a moment. Search your heart, and prayerfully consider if you are willing to play the part God has for you. For Mary, it meant the unspeakable joy of carrying Christ in her womb. For us, it means the inexplicable hope of hosting Christ in our hearts.

In addition to the account in the Bible, why not add at least one new story to your family's Christmas experience each year? You can find a wide variety of excellent stories at your favorite bookstore. Supplying your family with stories doesn't have to be expensive. If you're one for planning ahead, you can save significantly by shopping after-Christmas sales. You can also check out many Christmas classics like Charles Dickens's *A Christmas Carol* from your public library. Visit your church library, which can be a secret gold mine for Yuletide resources. Check local TV listings, and make a family night with popcorn to watch annual broadcasts of *A Charlie Brown Christmas* and *It's a Wonderful Life.* Last but not least, try rotating Christmas books and videos with your friends and neighbors to keep the new stories fresh and fun.

Being creative with your Christmas stories is guaranteed to be a lot of fun, and it might even increase the odds that your Christmas has a happy ending.

Remembering Stories

Think back to when you were a child. What were some of your favorite Christmas stories? Can you recall any of your parents' and grandparents' favorite tales?

_____

_____

_____

_____

_____

_____

_____

What were your favorite Christmas movies or TV specials when you were a child? What is your earliest memory of hearing or reading the Christmas Story of Scripture?

_____

_____

_____

_____

_____

_____

_____

_____

_____

How did you feel about it then? How has this changed now that you're an adult? _____

_____

_____

_____

_____

_____

_____

_____

Additional memories of Christmas stories: _____

_____

_____

_____

_____

_____

_____

_____

_____

_____

_____

_____

Remembering Stories

Over the years, your family will discover new Christmas stories and develop nostalgic affection for those that reappear annually as part of your family's annual Christmas tradition. Use the space below to record special stories or programs from that year and your memories of experiencing them as a family.

Christmas of the Year _____

_____

_____

_____

_____

_____

Christmas of the Year _____

_____

_____

_____

_____

_____

Christmas of the Year _____

_____

_____

_____

_____

Christmas of the Year _____

_____

_____

_____

_____

_____

Christmas of the Year _____

_____

_____

_____

_____

_____

Christmas of the Year _____

_____

_____

_____

_____

_____

The birth of Jesus

took place like this. His mother, Mary, was engaged to be married to Joseph. Before they came to the marriage bed, Joseph discovered she was pregnant. (It was by the Holy Spirit, but he didn't know that.) Joseph, chagrined but noble, determined to take care of things quietly so Mary would not be disgraced. While he was trying to figure a way out, he had a dream. God's angel spoke in the dream: "Joseph, son of David, don't hesitate to get married. Mary's pregnancy is Spirit-conceived. God's Holy Spirit has made her pregnant. She will bring a son to birth, and when she does, you, Joseph, will name him Jesus—'God saves'—because he will save his people from their sins." This would bring the prophet's embryonic sermon to full term: "Watch for this—a virgin will get pregnant and bear a son; They will name him Emmanuel" (Hebrew for "God is with us"). Then Joseph woke up. He did exactly what God's angel commanded in the dream: He married Mary. But he did not consummate the marriage until she had the baby. He named the baby Jesus.

—Matthew 1:18-25 THE MESSAGE

About that time Caesar Augustus ordered a census to be taken throughout the Empire. This was the first census when Quirinius was governor of Syria. Everyone had to travel to his own ancestral hometown to be accounted for. So Joseph went from the Galilean town of Nazareth up to Bethlehem in Judah, David's town, for the census. As a descendant of David, he had to go there. He went with Mary, his fiancée, who was pregnant. While they were there, the time came for her to give birth. She gave birth to a son, her firstborn. She wrapped him in a blanket and laid him in a manger, because there was no room in the hostel.

—Luke 2:1-7 THE MESSAGE

From our family to yours

Christmas Cards

Merry Christmas!

Wise men still seek Him

At that time Mary got ready and hurried
to a town in the hill country of Judea,
where she entered Zechariah's home
and greeted Elizabeth.
When Elizabeth heard Mary's greeting,
the baby leaped in her womb, and Elizabeth
was filled with the Holy Spirit.

—Luke 1:39-41

Signed, Sealed, Delivered.

*T*he daily routine of picking up the mail takes on a peculiarly positive tone around Christmas time. Perhaps that's because the onslaught of unwanted bills becomes peppered with bright envelopes bearing personal correspondence. Christmas cards are arriving!

The tradition of sending Yuletide greetings affords us the opportunity to turn our eyes from the tired stare at ourselves to peek in on the lives of our loved ones. Like a regularly scheduled appointment for catching up, these greetings remove the space from friends and family members who are separated by distance. Christmas letters condense the passing year into a simple summary. Christmas photos take up residence on the refrigerator, capturing a moment of the past for the days and months ahead.

The essence of a Christmas card, however, is not a family news bulletin or snapshot. It's a birth announcement. It's a declaration of a newborn's arrival. It's an invitation to share in the new joy and hope of a special new addition to our lives.

That was the impact of the very first Christmas greeting, given more than 2,000 years ago by Mary to her relative, Elizabeth. As soon as Mary learned that she and Elizabeth were both with child, she hurried to Zechariah's home in the hill country of Judea. When Elizabeth heard Mary's greeting, the baby leaped in her womb, and she was filled with the Holy Spirit. The greeting, the child, and the blessing were all tied together.

And so it remains today. Like Mary, we have a unique opportunity to proclaim the birth of the Savior with every Christmas greeting we send our friends and neighbors. Your cards are not merely a chance to keep in touch; they're an opportunity to touch lives for eternity with the message of the Messiah.

A Very Special Delivery

This year, before you immerse yourself in all the writing, licking, sealing, stamping, and addressing of your Christmas notes, reflect on the fact that Christmas is all about the arrival of a child. Do your cards demonstrate that? Think about the cards you'll choose before you buy them this year. Will they share the true hope of Christmas? Will they be noticed?

Why not make this year's Christmas card be like a birth announcement? Or get even more creative, and have your children draw a nativity scene that you can make color copies of and use as your Christmas card. Handmade Christmas cards from children are always adorable and fun to receive. The point is to make the message clear. You can still add updates or photos because news about your family is good. The Good News about Christ, however, is glorious. Together, they can make a meaningful greeting that brings joy and hope!

You can also use your Christmas cards to start a habit of praying together as a family. Save the cards in a basket, and beginning in January of the new year, read one card aloud at the dinner table. Then join hands as a family, and pray for the family that sent you the card. Work your way through the basket, and you'll find yourselves focusing on Christ long into the new year.

Remembering Cards

Think back to when you were a child. Did your parents send out Christmas cards?
Did they ever include pictures or newsletters?

_____

_____

_____

_____

_____

_____

_____

_____

What did your parents do with the Christmas cards they received? Were they put on display?
Were they shared with you at the table?

_____

_____

_____

_____

_____

_____

_____

_____

Record below any special memories you have of sending or receiving Christmas cards. What were your favorite greetings you received over the years and why?

_____

_____

_____

_____

_____

_____

_____

_____

_____

_____

_____

_____

_____

_____

_____

_____

_____

_____

_____

_____

_____

Remembering Cards

Each year, pick a personal favorite from the Christmas greetings you receive. Record who it was from and why you particularly enjoyed this correspondence. You might even keep one from each year right inside this book to preserve the memory.

Christmas of the Year _____

_____

_____

_____

_____

_____

Christmas of the Year _____

_____

_____

_____

_____

_____

Christmas of the Year _____

_____

_____

_____

_____

_____

Christmas of the Year _____

_____
_____
_____
_____
_____

Christmas of the Year _____

_____
_____
_____
_____
_____

Christmas of the Year _____

_____
_____
_____
_____
_____

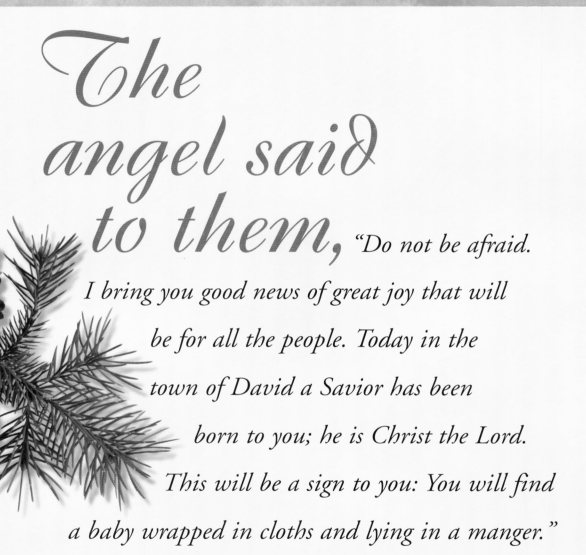

The angel said to them,

"Do not be afraid. I bring you good news of great joy that will be for all the people. Today in the town of David a Savior has been born to you; he is Christ the Lord. This will be a sign to you: You will find a baby wrapped in cloths and lying in a manger."

—Luke 2:10-12

*G*race and peace to you
from God our Father
and the Lord Jesus Christ.

—1 Corinthians 1:3

*G*reet one another with a holy kiss.
All the saints send their greetings.

—2 Corinthians 13:12

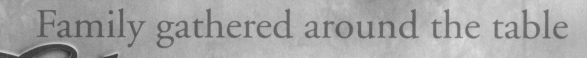

Family gathered around the table

Christmas Meals

Mouth-watering aromas

Candy canes and
gingerbread men

She gave birth to her firstborn, a son.
She wrapped him in cloths and placed him in a manger,
because there was no room for them in the inn.

—Luke 2:7

A Taste of Reality

These days, when a new baby is born, friends and family members demonstrate their support by dropping in with cards, flowers, and ready-to-eat meals. The couple can relax, confident that their bursting freezer will supply food throughout the uncertain days ahead. It's quite a different experience from that of Mary and Joseph.

Caesar Augustus issued a decree that a census should be taken to raise funds for the military. In other words, Joseph's taxes were due, and so was his fiancée's Baby. They had no choice but to leave their home town of Nazareth and travel the long journey to Bethlehem. As the Baby's delivery drew nearer, they were getting farther away from the familiar comforts of friends and family. They couldn't even get a room when they arrived in Bethlehem!

In the midst of this chaos, the Baby arrived. According to scripture, Mary wrapped her Newborn in cloths and placed Him in a manger. Based on this reference to a manger, scholars say He was born in a "stable." Contrary to most Christmas card depictions, the "stable" was most likely a dark and dirty cave with a few feeding troughs. It was not the expected surroundings of a King's birthplace.

On the first Christmas, rather than the scent of oven-roasted turkey and freshly baked cookies, the new parents' senses were surrounded by the stench of animal waste. No one was there to offer food for their table. In fact, they probably didn't have a table. Mary and Joseph probably shared their Newborn's hunger and made do with what they could find. To be sure, there was no feast that was fit for a King.

But that's not the end of the story. In fact, it's just the beginning. Christmas is the celebration of a special delivery—Baby who was born in the humblest of circumstances, but who now reigns in the riches of all glory. A Child who cried in hunger as a Newborn, but who now promises to satisfy all who hunger and thirst. He would be called the Bread of Life. And He would ask us to remember Him when we take the bread and the cup.

Because of Him, we are part of God's family. And that's worth celebrating with the best your kitchen can muster. So this year, before your family starts passing the pork roast and potatoes, pause a few moments to reflect on the awesome arrival of the One who fed the five thousand with five loaves and two small fish.

A Recipe for Fun

Does your family have a favorite Christmas cookie recipe? Even if you answered yes, who couldn't use a few more? And what could be better than the pursuit and production of the perfect Yuletide cookie? To find it, why not host a cookie exchange? Whether you've got an "ancient family secret" to share, or you're looking for new goodies to add to your collection, this is the perfect opportunity to enjoy the blessings of both giving and receiving.

Enlist your friends or office members to join in, and pick up a fun prize for the winner (such as a gift certificate to a local restaurant, book store, or movie theater). Since every participant ends up with a variety of different cookies and their recipes, everyone wins.

Start with a sign-up sheet that states the date, rules, and prize. Rules might include, "no store bought cookies," "no duplicate cookie types," and "no standard sugar, chocolate chip, or oatmeal cookies." When everyone has signed up, let the participants know how many cookies to make (based on each participant getting six or twelve cookies each). Remind them that they need to bring a copy of the recipe for each participant, along with the cookies to the taste test. Then let the baking begin.

You can let your office's visitors be the judges or do a secret ballot among the participants. Either way, you'll get a chance to taste a bunch of new recipes, have a lot of fun, and possibly put on a few holiday pounds early!

Remembering Meals

What were some of your favorite Christmas goodies your mother used to bake?

_____

_____

_____

_____

_____

_____

_____

What was the most unusual food you ever ate during the Christmas holiday?

_____

_____

_____

_____

_____

_____

_____

_____

_____

What are your favorite Christmas foods to prepare and eat?

Hot Beverage _____

Cold Beverage _____

Breakfast Item _____

Lunch Meal _____

Dinner Meal _____

Dessert _____

Snack _____

What (if any) ethnic foods were served in your family as part of a cultural tradition?
Which of those do you absolutely, positively not wish to continue?

_____

_____

_____

_____

_____

_____

Do you have a family secret recipe you want to preserve? Write it down here.

_____

_____

_____

_____

_____

_____

Remembering Meals

Over the years, your family will want to remember special memories of Christmas cuisine. Use the space below to record the year's food highlights and the memorable people who shared them with you.

Christmas of the Year _____

_____

_____

_____

_____

_____

Christmas of the Year _____

_____

_____

_____

_____

_____

Christmas of the Year _____

_____

_____

_____

_____

_____

Christmas of the Year _____

_____

_____

_____

_____

_____

Christmas of the Year _____

_____

_____

_____

_____

_____

Christmas of the Year _____

_____

_____

_____

_____

_____

Then Jesus declared, "I am the bread of life. He who comes to me will never go hungry, and he who believes in me will never be thirsty."

—John 6:35

Taste and see that the LORD is good.

—Psalm 34:8

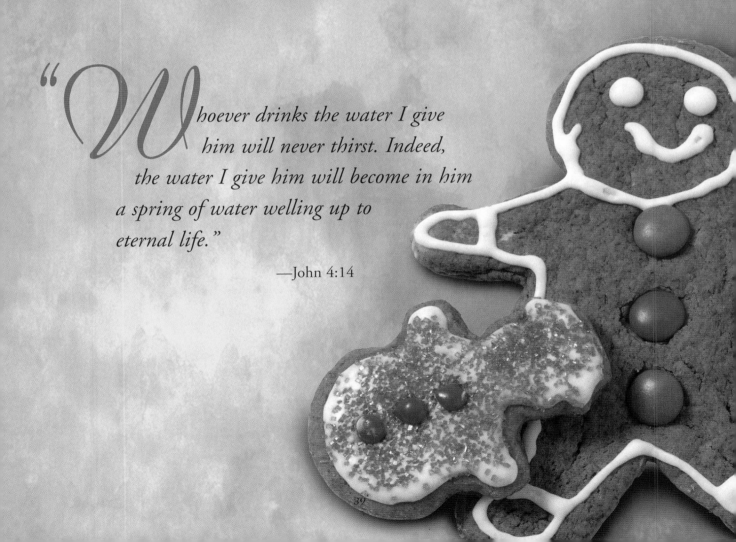

"*Blessed are you who hunger now,
for you will be satisfied.*"

—Luke 6:21

"*Whoever drinks the water I give
him will never thirst. Indeed,
the water I give him will become in him
a spring of water welling up to
eternal life.*"

—John 4:14

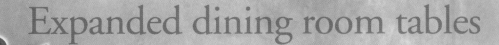

Expanded dining room tables

Christmas Guests

Eager trips to
the airport

Freshly made beds

The shepherds returned, glorifying and

praising God for all the

things they had

heard and seen,

which were

just as they

had been told.

—Luke 2:20

A Welcome Reminder

Christmas is the busiest travel time of the year. The airports, bus stations, and freeways are all crammed with people frantically attempting to unite with their friends and family. Traffic jams, flight delays, airport closures, and oversold trips all threaten to deplete our reserve of Christmas joy before we reach our destination.

But even when the distance to be traveled isn't very far, the tendency for tension can still be tremendous. Trying to calm wild kids before guests arrive can be futile and frustrating. Icy roads can turn a winter wonderland into a white-knuckled stress ride. And fleeting fears about potential problems with the meals, gifts, decorations, planned events, and sleeping arrangements can set you on a crash course for discouragement.

But having guests in your home over the holidays doesn't have to be a source of strain—even if you're not too excited about who is coming to dinner. It can actually be a genuine source of inspiration for you and your guests, as long as you keep in mind what's important for them to see. It's not what you have to offer, but how you offer it that makes your hospitality special.

After all, the goal is not to create a magical, make-believe environment that radiates perfection. Rather, the objective is to make it easy for your guests to see Christ. That's what Mary and Joseph did. That was all they could do, and it was more than enough.

Mary and Joseph were a long, long way from home when their Baby was born. Nobody extended hospitality to them. There was no room at the inn, so they had to stay out. And they weren't staying in a cozy guest room or cottage; they were sleeping in a stable. Jesus wasn't nuzzled beneath a warm blanket or dressed up in a special outfit. He was wrapped in strips of cloth, almost like a mummy, and laid in a feeding trough. They could not have been less prepared (emotionally or materially) to receive visitors.

But the uninvited guests came. The first to arrive were shepherds, who, socially speaking, were close to the status of lepers. Many regarded these poor and dirty workers as thieves. And yet this couple had nothing worth stealing, except a glimpse of the Savior—the very reason they came.

When the shepherds left, they weren't talking about how nice the stable was or how good the food was. But make no mistake, they couldn't stop talking. They were praising and glorifying God and spreading the word of all they had seen and heard.

Later, when the wealthy and wise Magi came, bearing precious gifts of gold, incense, and myrrh, Mary still probably felt like a miserably meager hostess. Joseph probably felt like an embarrassingly inadequate provider. Yet despite their feelings, they welcomed these visitors, as well, then gave what they had to offer—a closer look at the Lord. And that's what having guests at Christmas is all about—helping those who have come to visit, see the Christ in Christmas.

When you have friends and family in your home, try not to get consumed in the details. Rather, let yourself be consumed by Christ's birth. The most meaningful journey people take is not from their home to yours. It's in discovering Jesus' birth in the manger, His death on the cross, and His resurrection from the tomb. By making Christ the focus of your family's Christmas celebration, you can help them complete the journey of knowing Him as Lord and Savior.

Open Invitation

Christmas is a time to be creative! You can implement family traditions that help keep Jesus the central Figure of the holiday season in your home. Here are a some ideas:

- Set an extra place setting at the table when you have special holiday meals. When people ask who it is for, you can tell them it is a place setting reserved for Jesus, who has been invited into your home for Christmas.

- Serve a birthday cake for dessert at your main holiday meal. Have your children answer the question of whose birthday you're celebrating and then let them blow out the candles.

- Help your children find props around the house for use in putting on their own Christmas play. Ask your guest to read the Christmas Story aloud while the children act out the parts.

- At the dinner table, talk about the Christmas Story and what it must have been like to be a part of it. How would it have felt to have been Mary? Or Joseph? Or one of the shepherds? What would have been going through your mind if you were one of the characters?

- When everyone is gathered around the table, say a special prayer of thanks to God, not only for the food and family gathered, but also for sending His Son to save the world. Invite those around the table to join hands and also pray if they feel led, then give them an opportunity to pray out loud or silently before you finish saying grace.

- Send your guests home with a handmade ornament. You can decorate globes with paint pens or glue and glitter to read "Christmas at the _____'s" (use your last name). Don't forget to add the year. In the future, your guests will recall their time with your family when they decorate their own tree.

Remembering Guests

Ask your guests to sign this section whenever you host visitors at Christmas.

Date	Name	Message from Guest

Remembering Guests

Date	Name	Message from Guest

Date	Name	Message from Guest

Remembering Guests

Date	Name	Message from Guest

Date   Name   Message from Guest

Remembering Guests

Date	Name	Message from Guest

Date   Name   Message from Guest

When the angels had left them and gone into heaven, the shepherds said to one another,

"Let's go to Bethlehem and see this thing that has happened, which the Lord has told us about." So they hurried off and found Mary and Joseph, and the baby, who was lying in the manger. When they had seen him, they spread the word concerning what had been told them about this child, and all who heard it were amazed at what the shepherds said to them.

—Luke 2:15-18

*O*ffer hospitality to one another
without grumbling.

—1 Peter 4:9

*S*hare with God's people
who are in need. Practice hospitality.

—Romans 12:13

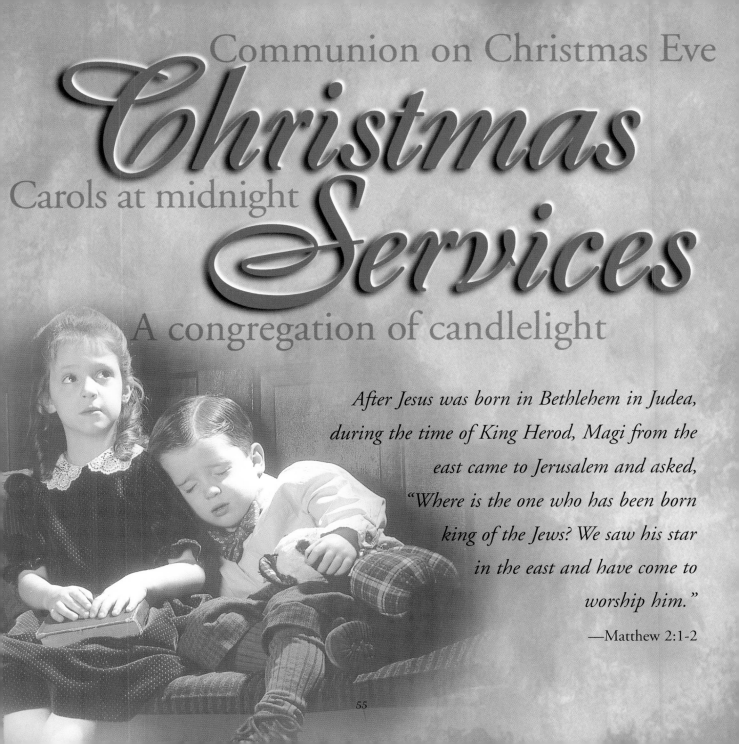

Communion on Christmas Eve

Christmas

Carols at midnight

Services

A congregation of candlelight

After Jesus was born in Bethlehem in Judea, during the time of King Herod, Magi from the east came to Jerusalem and asked, "Where is the one who has been born king of the Jews? We saw his star in the east and have come to worship him."

—Matthew 2:1-2

A
Touching
Service

No matter how frigid the air is, the youngest and oldest hearts are warmed in the safety of a sanctuary on Christmas Eve. This is a special gathering. Folks from across the country have reunited with their families, and they now huddle closely in their pews. The regulars are here, but so are many new faces. Friends, neighbors, and church members alike have come together for a special evening of reflection and rejoicing.

Christmas Eve service—what better place to escape the stress of holiday hassles and focus on the Reason for the season! Amidst the clamor of crying babies and coughing adults, you can still find a special stillness—a quiet place to ponder the wonder of it all . . . and be touched.

It might happen as you pensively partake in communion. Or as you lean over and light the stubby wax candle held by the person next to you. Or as the pastor passionately concludes the moving message. Suddenly you're not thinking about unruly relatives, hospitality hassles, or aggravating sleeping arrangements. Instead, you're thinking about a miracle that took place in Bethlehem. Christ the Lord has come. Born of a Virgin Mary. Just as was foretold.

Suddenly, the familiar refrains of Christmas carols you've sung since you were a child are alive and exciting. Suddenly, your voice is a vehicle for offering up praise. Suddenly, Christmas isn't about what you have to do. It's about what you want to do—come and worship the newborn King. You share the mission of the Magi. And as the service concludes and you step out into the night air, you can't help but notice a star in the sky that shines brighter than the others.

A wondrous awakening awaits us all. This Christmas, be like the Magi. Come looking for God when you come to church on Christmas Eve. Hang on to hope, and follow His leading. You don't have to travel as far as the Magi to discover the same joy in coming face to face with the Lord, and neither do your friends, relatives, and neighbors. Why not invite them all to your Christmas Eve service? God can meet them—and us—in His house on Christmas Eve.

Remembering Services

Did you attend Christmas Eve services when you were a child?
What do you remember about them?

_____

_____

_____

_____

_____

_____

What was your favorite part of the service?

_____

_____

_____

_____

As you grew older, how did your perspective on the service change?

_____

_____

_____

_____

How does your church celebrate Christmas? With a midnight service? A special communion ceremony? A candlelight chorus? A Christmas pageant? A living nativity?

_____

_____

_____

_____

_____

_____

_____

_____

What are some of your best memories of Christmas Eve services over the years? Where did they take place?

_____

_____

_____

_____

_____

_____

_____

_____

_____

_____

_____

Remembering Services

Use this space to record special memories of Christmas Eve services in the years to come. Be sure to note where you were that year and who accompanied you to the service.

Christmas of the Year _____

_____

_____

_____

_____

_____

Christmas of the Year _____

_____

_____

_____

_____

_____

Christmas of the Year _____

_____

_____

_____

_____

_____

Christmas of the Year _____

_____

_____

_____

_____

Christmas of the Year _____

_____

_____

_____

_____

Christmas of the Year _____

_____

_____

_____

_____

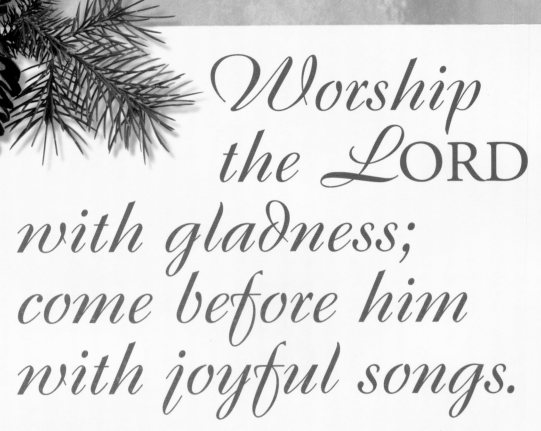

Worship the LORD

with gladness;
come before him
with joyful songs.

—Psalm 100:2

Let us not give up meeting together, as some are in the habit of doing, but let us encourage one another—and all the more as you see the Day approaching.

—Hebrews 10:25

You are no longer foreigners and aliens, but fellow citizens with God's people and members of God's household, built on the foundation of the apostles and prophets, with Christ Jesus himself as the chief cornerstone. In him the whole building is joined together and rises to become a holy temple in the Lord.

—Ephesians 2:19-21

Angels we have heard on high

Christmas

O little town

Carols

Par rum pum pum pum

When they saw the star,
they were overjoyed.
On coming to the house,
they saw the child
with his mother
Mary, and they
bowed down and
worshiped him.

—Matthew 2:10-11

Joy
to the
World

Christmas is one of those rare times when exuberance is more valuable than execution—especially when it comes to singing! Perhaps that's because Christmas carols are not about singing in the perfect pitch. They're about worshiping from the heart.

As we gather in our pews and stroll from door to door, we are taking part in a declaration and a celebration. We are recognizing that, despite the humble appearances on the evening of His birth, a King has come into the land and into our lives.

This is a King whose impossible conception makes it possible for us to be born again. Whose delivery means we can be delivered from sin. Whose birth allows us to die to ourselves. And whose death makes it possible for us to live forever.

Because of Joseph and Mary's Son, we have gained the right to become children of our Heavenly Father, and we are heirs to His riches and glory! Now that's worth singing about, even if you can't carry a tune!

Caroling, Caroling

Singing Christmas carols in your community is far more than a nostalgic notion. It's a special opportunity to preserve the true meaning of Christmas in our material culture. It's also a creative way to share the greatest story ever told in song. This is a never-ending story that begins in the manger, pauses at the cross, and continues on in the heavens and our hearts.

When we sing carols, we declare the good news that Christ has come! From "What Child Is This?" and "We Three Kings" to "Silent Night" and "God Rest Ye Merry Gentleman," songs like these are both inspirational and integral to the American Christmas tradition. They are a wonderful heritage to be passed on for future generations to enjoy.

This Christmas, why not take your kids caroling? It could just be around the block. Or around the office. Or you could visit an elderly home, hospice care facility, or homeless shelter. Make an effort to share the joy and music of Christmas with others. Even if you can't get out this year, you can make them a part of your children's bedtime. Our Christmas carols are simply too delightful to confine within the walls of church.

Remembering Carols

What were your favorite Christmas carols when you were a child? What did you like about them?

_____

_____

_____

_____

_____

_____

_____

_____

What are your favorite Christmas carols as an adult?

_____

_____

_____

_____

_____

_____

_____

_____

_____

What Christmas songs do your children particularly enjoy?

_____

_____

_____

_____

_____

_____

_____

_____

What are your family's favorite Christmas recordings to play around the holiday?

_____

_____

_____

_____

_____

_____

_____

_____

Away In a Manger

Away in a manger no crib for a bed;

The little Lord Jesus lay down His sweet head.

The stars in the sky looked down where He lay;

The little Lord Jesus asleep on the hay.

The cattle are lowing the baby awakes;

But little Lord Jesus no crying He makes.

I love Thee, Lord Jesus, look down from the sky;

And stay by my cradle till morning is nigh.

Be near me, Lord Jesus, I ask Thee to stay;

Close by me forever and love me I pray.

Bless all the dear children in Thy tender care;

And fit us for heaven to live with Thee there.

Silent Night

Silent night, holy night,
All is calm, all is bright.
Round yon virgin mother and child;
Holy infant, so tender and mild,
Sleep in heavenly peace;
Sleep in heavenly peace.

Silent night, holy night,
Darkness flies, all is light;
Shepherds hear the angels sing,
"Alleluia! Hail the King!
Christ the Savior is born;
Christ the Savior is born."

Silent night, holy night,
Son of God, love's pure light.
Radiant beams from Thy holy face,
With the dawn of redeeming grace.
Jesus, Lord, at Thy birth;
Jesus, Lord, at Thy birth.

Silent night, holy night,
Wondrous star, lend thy light.
With the angels, let us sing,
Alleluia to our King.
Christ the Savior is born;
Christ the Savior is born.

Speak to one another
with psalms, hymns and
spiritual songs.
Sing and make music
in your heart to the LORD,
always giving thanks to
God the Father for
everything, in the name of
our LORD Jesus Christ.

—Ephesians 5:19-20

*G*lory to God in the highest,
and on earth peace to men
on whom his favor rests.

—Luke 2:14

*C*ome, let us bow down
in worship.

—Psalm 95:6

*W*orship the LORD with gladness;
come before him with joyful songs.

—Psalm 100:2

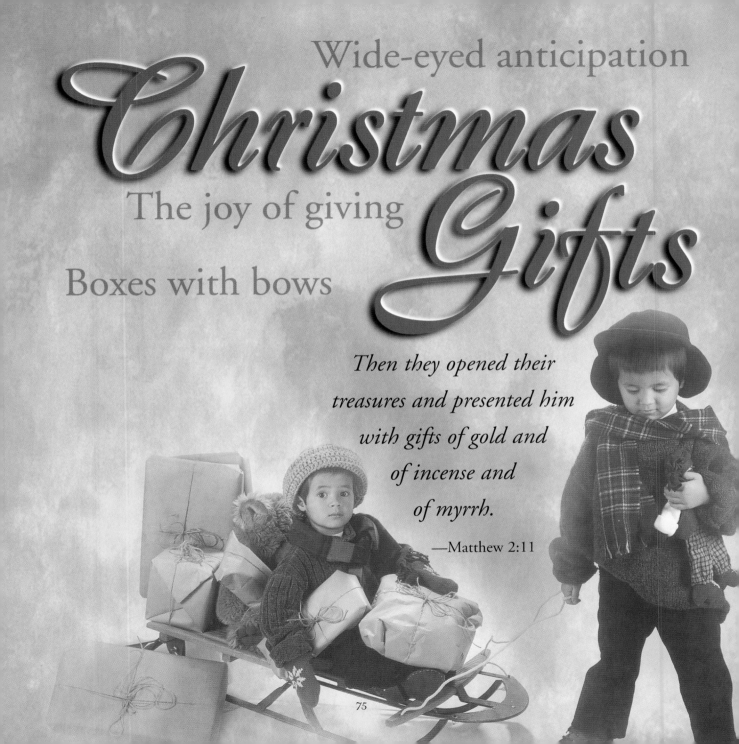

Wide-eyed anticipation

Christmas Gifts

The joy of giving

Boxes with bows

*Then they opened their
treasures and presented him
with gifts of gold and
of incense and
of myrrh.*

—Matthew 2:11

Our Finest Gifts We Bring...

*I*n today's commercially crazed culture, the pursuit of presents has pushed its way to the forefront of our thoughts. Each year, it becomes a little more difficult to put the manger before the mall. But if we pause to ponder the earliest Christmas gifts that were given, we discover a heart-warming reminder of what Christmas is really all about.

Long before we began wrapping packages in colorful metallic paper, a Child was wrapped in drab swaddling clothes. Before our trees held ornaments, a wooden manger held a Child. Before festive and decorative lights illuminated our homes, a star that rose in the East illuminated the way to a Child.

This was a special Child. Born of a Virgin. Born to be a King. Born to Die . . . and save us from our sin. Jesus was the first and greatest Gift ever given.

The very first Christmas Gift was perfect—one size fits all. We could never outgrow It. Or break It. Or lose It. It would last forever. Although It was costly, It was given freely. From the heart of God. For the hearts of all people.

Some time after the first gift was given, a journey was nearing completion. Led by a star that rose from the East, the Magi came searching for a Child who would be King. Their very presence was a precious gift of faith. They covered many miles with no map, compass, or travel guide. All they had to go by was a blazing light in the sky. In faith, they came to Jesus.

And when they found Him, they gave another gift— their praise. They bowed their heads and lifted their hearts. After offering their worship, they offered their treasures. Scripture tells us they presented the Child with gifts of gold, incense, and myrrh. These precious gifts proclaim the uniqueness of Christ. Gold was a gift given to a king. Incense was a gift offered up to deity, and myrrh was a spice for a man who was going to die. The gifts were personal and remarkable. Just like the One they were given to.

This year, when you're shopping for presents, consider the origin of the custom. The first and best gifts were gifts of the heart. Their personal value was far superior to their financial worth. And most importantly, they were designed to draw attention to—not distract from—the arrival of our Lord and Savior.

Gifts of the Heart

You don't have to spend a fortune to celebrate the Savior. Christmas joy can be spread without a credit card. In fact, you and your family may want to intentionally choose creativity over the customary to keep Jesus the center of your Christmas gift-giving celebration. The possibilities are endless, but here are a couple of ideas to consider:

• Make coupon books for friends and family members that can be "cashed in" for gifts of your time, such as baby-sitting, car washing, lawn mowing, dog walking, grocery shopping, dining at your home—whatever would be meaningful to the specific receiver.

• Make a donation to a charitable organization in the honor of the person whom you wish to give a gift. (Be sure it's an organization the person you're honoring feels good about). Make a personal card that explains the contribution you've given in his or her honor and how it will help others.

• Bake a batch of your best cookies, and deliver them to friends, along with a hand-made recipe card.

• Shop for inexpensive ornaments you can personalize with a paint pen, glue, and glitter. Write the year and "With Love" on it, and sign your name. You can photocopy pictures to give them a classic black and white look and then glue them to the ornament.

• Make your own wrapping paper. Using white tissue paper and crayons, cover the surface with Christmas greetings, your children's Christmas drawings, and cutouts from Christmas catalogs.

• Encourage your kids to write thank-you notes on the same day they open their Christmas gifts, perhaps even include a drawing of them playing with the toy (while the excitement is still running high). Their notes will be treasured by the recipients.

Remembering Gifts

Think back to when you were a child. Can you recall the anticipation and excitement of unwrapping presents? What were some of your favorite Christmas gifts you received? Whom were they from?

_____

_____

_____

_____

_____

_____

When were you most excited about giving a gift to someone else? Whom was it for? What was the gift?

_____

_____

_____

_____

_____

_____

_____

Describe the most thoughtful or personal gift anyone has ever given you.

_____

_____

_____

_____

_____

_____

_____

_____

_____

_____

_____

_____

_____

_____

_____

_____

_____

_____

Remembering Gifts

Over the years, your family will want to hold on to special memories of gifts given and received. Use the space below to record each year's gift-giving highlights and the memorable stories and people behind them.

Christmas of the Year _____

_____

_____

_____

_____

Christmas of the Year _____

_____

_____

_____

_____

Christmas of the Year _____

_____

_____

_____

_____

Christmas of the Year _____

_____

_____

_____

_____

_____

Christmas of the Year _____

_____

_____

_____

_____

_____

Christmas of the Year _____

_____

_____

_____

_____

_____

"For God
so loved the world
that He gave
his one and only Son,
that whoever believes
in Him shall not perish
but have eternal life."

—John 3:16

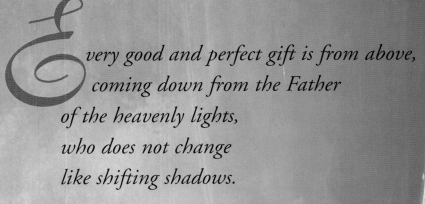

*E*very good and perfect gift is from above,
coming down from the Father
of the heavenly lights,
who does not change
like shifting shadows.

—James 1:17

*T*hanks be to God
for his indescribable gift!

—2 Corinthians 9:15

Hanging the stockings

Christmas Traditions

Unpacking the nativity

Lighting the tree

Then Simeon blessed them and said to Mary, his mother: "This child is destined to cause the falling and rising of many in Israel, and to be a sign that will be spoken against, so that the thoughts of many hearts will be revealed."

—Luke 2:34-35

Keeping the Traditions

*O*ver the years, a tremendous variety of traditions have found their way into our Christmas celebrations. Some are part of a rich, cultural heritage. Some are unique and personal to individual families. Some are rooted in faith. And some are simply fun.

In New Mexico, it is a popular Christmas Eve tradition to set out brown paper bags with sand in the bottom and a small candle inside. The bags are set out along driveways, walkways, and rooftops. These "luminarias" create a spectacular glow in the evenings. The custom originated in the sixteenth century, when small bonfires were lit alongside roads and churchyards to commemorate the birth of Christ and to guide people to midnight mass.

In Colorado, one man strings a series of lights on his roof to form the letter "L" inside a circle with a "restricted" diagonal line across the letter. Due to the hills of the area, his lights can be seen from quite a distance. The bright symbol has caused numerous chuckles as puzzled onlookers ask and answer the question at the same time, "NO L?" (Noel!)

An American family serving as missionaries in Russia unpacks their nativity set on December 1 and has the children scatter most of the characters throughout the house. Each night before bed, the children move Mary and Joseph closer to the stable. On Christmas morning, the parents place the baby Jesus in the manger, so the children wake to see Him lying there. Later that evening, the children bring the shepherds and Magi in to pay their respects.

Hanging wreaths on the door, ornaments on the tree, lights on the roof, and stockings on the fireplace are fun Christmas traditions for families. But they do far more than merely entertain us. They give us a strong sense of stability. It's comforting to know we can always count on certain things.

Children benefit tremendously from the sensation of security and belonging when there is routine in their lives. And the same is true for adults. Traditions give all of us something to look forward to, something to eagerly anticipate. There is tremendous joy in seeing promises for the future kept. Sometimes, we even catch a glimpse of God at work in the process. Simeon did.

Keeping the Faith

A righteous and devout man, Simeon had been promised by the Holy Spirit that he would not die before he had seen the Lord's Christ. The Spirit drew him to the temple courts in Jerusalem. A cultural tradition drew Mary, Joseph, and Jesus to the same place. The Jews had specific customs they followed when a baby was born. Firstborn children were to be presented to God in the temple. Women who had sons were not considered "clean" until forty days after the birth. Once this time had elapsed, the couple were to bring two animal sacrifices as part of the purification ceremony.

Mary and Joseph were carrying out these traditions. Simeon was seeing the Lord at work—seeing the Lord himself in the flesh. What an incredible experience! This was the moment he had literally been living for. Now he could die in peace.

Simeon told Mary her Child was special. And he delivered a prediction that came true. "This child is destined to cause the falling and rising of many in Israel, and to be a sign that will be spoken against, so that the thoughts of many hearts will be revealed." Even to this day, Jesus forces us to look at the content of our hearts.

God is constantly at work around us, and most of the time we don't even realize that He is orchestrating events to keep His Word. The entire Christmas Story is a remarkable series of promises being fulfilled. The Old Testament foretold of Jesus being a Descendent of David (Jeremiah 33:15), born in Bethlehem (Micah 5:2), and born of a virgin (Isaiah 7:14). Jesus fulfilled these prophecies and many, many others.

The same book that told of His birth also tells of His return. It is another promise we can count on being fulfilled. It is a reason for hope. It is something to prepare for and look forward to year round, and it is more important than any tradition we enjoy during this holiday.

Remembering Traditions

What Christmas traditions did your family celebrate when you were a child? What did you look forward to most every year?

_____

_____

_____

_____

_____

_____

_____

What traditions were popular in the community you grew up? Were there city-wide celebrations or cultural customs that took place in your area?

_____

_____

_____

_____

_____

_____

_____

_____

What things were particularly unique about the way your family celebrated Christmas?

_____

_____

_____

_____

_____

_____

_____

Describe the most interesting Christmas tradition you have ever heard about.

_____

_____

_____

_____

_____

_____

_____

_____

_____

_____

Remembering Traditions

What Christmas celebrations have you and your spouse "carried on" from your own families?

_____

_____

_____

_____

_____

_____

_____

What new or unique traditions have you started with your own children?

_____

_____

_____

_____

_____

_____

_____

_____

_____

What traditions would you most hope your children would pass on to their children?

_____

_____

_____

_____

_____

_____

_____

_____

What single tradition helps your family reflect on Christ the most? Why?

_____

_____

_____

_____

_____

_____

_____

_____

_____

Now there was a man in Jerusalem called Simeon, who was righteous and devout. He was waiting for the consolation of Israel, and the Holy Spirit was upon him. It had been revealed to him by the Holy Spirit that he would not die before he had seen the Lord's Christ. Moved by the Spirit, he went into the temple courts. When the parents brought in the child Jesus to do for him what the custom of the Law required, Simeon took him in his arms and praised God.

—Luke 2:25-28

"*I have come that they may have life, and have it to the full.*"

—John 10:10

"*Therefore keep watch, because you do not know on what day your LORD will come.*"

—Matthew 24:42

Sentimental REFLECTIONS

For a closer look at the complete line of
Sentimental Reflections resources, please
visit www.sentimentalreflections.com

Additional copies of this

book and other titles in the

Sentimental Reflections series

are available from your

local bookstore.

HB HONOR BOOKS

Please contact us at:
Honor Books
Department E
P.O. Box 55388
Tulsa, Oklahoma 74155
Or by e-mail at:
info@honorbooks.com